VANCOUVER: A POEM

▼

VANCOUVER: A POEM

George Stanley

VANCOUVER ▼ NEW STAR BOOKS ▼ 2009

NEW STAR BOOKS LTD.

107 — 3477 Commercial Street, Vancouver, BC V5N 4E8   CANADA
1574 Gulf Road, No. 1517, Point Roberts, WA 98281   USA
www.NewStarBooks.com   info@NewStarBooks.com

Publication of this work is made possible by the support of the
Government of Canada through the Canada Council and the
Department of Canadian Heritage Book Publishing Industry
Development Fund, and the Province of British Columbia
through the British Columbia Arts Council and the Book
Publishing Tax Credit.

Cover by Mutasis.com
Cover image: Roy Arden — *Cordova Street, Vancouver
B.C.* (1995). Courtesy Roy Arden and Monte Clark Gallery,
Vancouver/Toronto.
Printed on 100% post-consumer recycled paper
Printed and bound in Canada by Gauvin Press
First published 2008. Reprinted 2009

LIBRARY AND ARCHIVES CANADA
CATALOGUING IN PUBLICATION

Stanley, George, 1934–
    Vancouver : a poem / George Stanley.

ISBN 978-1-55420-038-2
    1. Vancouver (B.C.) — Poetry.   I. Title.
PS8587.T3232V35 2008   C811'.54   C2008–900355–1

VANCOUVER: A POEM

▼

1

▼

There is more here than memory.

▼

Reading *Paterson* on the bus, back & forth. Across the city. The 210. A man & a city.

I am not a man & this is not my city.

Williams though as a guide. His universals as particulars, ideas in things. His rhythms. Ever rhythmic, shaking (like a belly-dancer), splashing (like the Falls) lines. Insistences. Insistence on persisting. Oh, maybe that, yes. But to take the thing to its . . . or maybe come back & find it later. Seasonal. Recurrences. And something else 'out of the blue' with a certainty (but I have no certainty) that the fact of it ('of it,' that's Williams) — might —

Vertigo. Vair to go?

(Student comes up to my desk with woeful expression. 'I forgot to double space. Should I start over?' 'No. Double space now.')

Reading him back & forth on the bus, the 210, & also reading him forth, & then back, back to the beginning of some 'poem' — in the larger poem, some break, impetus — of thought — & perception — pent up, while it seems he is *reading* the prose passages he has written, reading ahead, reading a newspaper, or in the library, page of an almanac, memoir, time before his childhood, turns the page —

& his mind takes off, & so much of it (there's that 'of it' again
— lost it there — students handing in papers) — somewhere
there's coloured petals (paper after paper lights on the pile) — or
something like fruits, flowers, lights, held up, & dancing in the
fountain — they come from everywhere — & this is the point
— from anywhere — the *it* is large enough — you see, it's all —

Watching it go by on the bus, even — that's relativity — I mean
watching me go by — the city. So a catalogue of moments,
glimpses — no, just a disconnected (I imagine a poem about
Vancouver in which Vancouver never appears — no, I mean *no
glimpses* — Vancouver only in the mind of — trying to let it be,
thinking that if (& what about the subject position? that revealed
coyly, or just blurted out?) Thinking that if — no glimpses, but
the first thing glimpsed would open the way for (some idea of
rubble here, rubbies?) — the way — the diagonal — / the tracks
/ — extending from the CP main line (careful, watch it!) through
Gastown, across Hastings at Carrall (this is like Saint-Henri
in *The Tin Flute*, train tracks crossing the people's street — an
account of all (oh, some) of the many times, ways, this (subject
position) crossed, or stayed on the same side of the street (coyly,
letting no one know who he was), or crossed & went through
Army & Navy, beginning that catalogue, rubble — or

V is for Victory Square — IS IT NOTHING TO YOV?
— glimpsed first I guess on a pub crawl, with Dennis Forkin &
Evert Hoogers —

(Something about 'The Masses' — an institutional ad high on the
wall of Army & Navy. Tony Tryyard phoned up the head office —
not sure why — trying to sell them an ad in the *Grape*? — made
some reference to that sign — the guy said, 'Aw, that was put up

4

years ago' — disclaimed — any connection — to 'The Masses'

(When did they — cease to be? Timothy Garton Ash saw them in Budapest around 1990 — just after the Wall fell — they were funny-looking — big noses, faces that bulged — they didn't all look the same — coats & ties on workers) —

Pub crawls started on Main ('In all the beer parlours, all down along Main Street'). It feels like it would be Saturday morning — in the Fall — start of the school year — denial of that — transgression. The American, The Cobalt (dyke) — & there was one in Chinatown, too, was it Pender & Gore? *The Stratford!* — & then back down Pender & around the corner onto Hastings. One glass (20¢) or small (10¢) at each —

Stuck stuck stuck the W — a poem in the new *Sulfur* began with a quote from Bréton that the surrealists opposed the W to the V of the visible —

The W atop Woodward's — the big, brick, block-long (almost — next building west was Woolworth's — another W (west a W, was a W) — the Food Floor — little restaurant behind, lunch counter (like where Florentine worked) — the polished oak framed glass doors — two sets — a vestibule — or just a space between — push, to open — dark on Cordova — & now fear, or anxiety, at winter — getting older, but that's — not adequate — snow — yes, but don't try to describe — feelings — the Parkade across the street — now empty — Woodward's boarded up — a big development sign — black on white — a placard, with a diagram of the block — too high to read, to deter graffiti — & warnings of dogs. Then the windows — Christmas displays — angels twirling on canes & animals' mouths opened — did the Bay take them — are they the same ones (I hear Margaret Laurence's voice in that 'same') — & the snow & so many old people, some bent over, carrying shopping bags — always some kind of avoidance

          not to be a man,
          to be a thought
struggling through snow, carrying — not to care about the meaning — plod

          stuck stuck stuck what kind of feeling down in Woodward's basement on a Saturday morning buying fresh ground peanut butter, then a cup of soup & a toasted tuna & a Coke, sitting at the counter — the women in their uniforms — brown & tan — did — word by word — plod — safety — always felt in the past —

Upstairs buying pants, I said to the tailor, 'The woman was showing me a pair,' & he (by the racks of pants) replied, 'She's a lady' — emphasizing *his* past, gentility — & I'm trying to drag him back into an earlier past — well only slightly earlier — 'The Masses' —

Still in that space between the doors — of Woodward's. Back door, steps coming down from the main floor, or up from the basement — the Food Floor. Polished oak frames of the doors — glass. Warm in here, looking out at the snow — there are hard rubber mats attached to the hardwood floor — to knock the snow off — wet snow falling fast in streaks, against the darkness. The dark shape of the Parkade, across the street, filled with cars (now empty). Waiting for — feeling safe — image of finger to lips as if something not to be said. Stuck stuck stuck stuck stuck stuck stuck the pub crawl goes by on the other side of the — trying too hard to think — store — Hastings — the W rises on its little Eiffel Tower — the W seen from the other side of the inlet — red, turning slowly — from the Seabus — turn-of-the-century façade of warehouses — feelings without words about places —

like driving (so many times) from Berkeley across the Bay Bridge to SF in the early evening — Friday — & seeing the lights going on up the streets on Nob Hill — red & blue spots of cocktail bars at the corners — & thinking, there's something there for me — there's life —

but this is different, I'm almost cowering in the space between the doors of Woodward's — afraid to go out — as if some terrible thing, some terror, was coming (& not assuming any knowledge) over the city, low buildings to the west, behind the snow — that to go out would be

the beginning of knowing this city

& the different Canadians, their minds, that patience, waiting for me to finish (as now) my account of what it was like.

That's finished, that's what it was like, now let's have supper. Lamps from second-hand stores. A different sense of time, of events, here, as discrete, not overlapping.

But out there in the night, other. Other than being here, in the city. And close.

And outer.

2

▼

The W

turned against the sky
like a reminder
of people of people

The W

turned against the sky, impersonal
reminder of a certain way of life, people
envisioning people, not merely plural

Like the Lions, & like the twin piles
of sulfur on the North Shore

The W

turned in the air like an X-
mas star, a reminder
of people as people

(like the hills of sulfur mean nothing
except that it falls so (we fall so)

like the Lions (up the canyon)
are rock as human

But the people as people
thronging the streets, post-war

in search not so much of luxuries
as of attractive (or acceptable) necessities
to continue
living in a golden age,

as it seems now to us
knowing it was not to you.

You gave it authority,
though it crippled you.

My students,
thinking us '60s softies hard
on them, but soft on us,
on our own style of idleness,
know neither of our
displacement
nor of your devotion.

Crossing Burrard Inlet
& passing between
mountainous freighters
& cyclopean sea-cranes

The W
        turned,
                turned against the sky
like a reminder of people of people.

Turned against life, against death,
against mortality, eternity,
turned, turned.

(& in this era of vegetarian pizza,
disappearance of the Government, & of the People)

▼

Like the Lions, before I came,
ran out on the field
to roar in '54
at Empire Stadium
where Roger Bannister & John Landy ran the mile.

The W
          wasn't turning,
                              wasn't
there.

'The Woodward's Beacon was a 2 million candlepower rotating
searchlight perched on an Eiffel Tower-like structure built atop
Woodward's department store in 1927. The beam from this well-
known landmark could be seen from as far away as Chilliwack.
In the late 1950s the light was replaced by its present 5-metre (16
foot) high, red neon 'W.''

Not like the Q,
the swizzle stick at the Quay,
or Park Royal,
'Becoming more like you
every day.'

▼

I have a vision of
a place, light shifting,
night & day, where Earle Birney's
'Vancouver Lights' is read
down
from the North Shore
into a bottomless pit.

▼

The W turned
toward the sky,
the depths of the sky

The hills of sulfur
mean nothing
except that we fall so

The Lions are human rock,
wanting
to move forward, to prance

▼

As Landy & Bannister
are men of bronze

human bronze

as Bannister passed Landy
that day

Landy & Bannister were of us
(who wrote that, 'of us'?)

'Bannister shot past Landy'
(not to my knowledge, I was someone else,
a soldier in Arkansas)

& Terry Fox
was of us

& Steve Fonyo
at least
is not postmodern

▼

Who were we?
The ones that got dirty
or, fanatically, stayed clean

(But we all got 'dressed up'
to go downtown
on the cars, on Saturday)
Who were we?

▼

They have to shop
at the Chinese stores
where they can't read the language
since the Food Floor closed

3

▼

Landmarks. One of them of course is beneath
the horizon, west or south, however you put it.

▼

The mountains behind the North Shore. The Lions.

We see two rocks, & call them Lions,
the heads & manes bare in summer;
in winter the snow on their sides
suggests the whole bodies, couchant,

& we think of them like dogs — even like bears —
hold them blameless.

▼

To see the sun through the murk of ideologies —
pollution over the city, flows from west to east —
is a haze indistinguishable from memory.

In the valley of the shadow of death —
& then it doesn't seem like a valley —
it's a street — in Britain a *high street* —
Fourth Avenue, on a height with a higher
hill to the west — a finger of the Arbutus Ridge —
& looking west to University Hill,
the sun at the equinoxes, spring & fall

sets due west (or close to it)
& dazzles the eye — in late afternoon —
cuts through the ideologies that say
I'm meant for something else — some fixity —
(reflection on reflection — in the windows
of Book Warehouse) —

go down with this sun the voice says,
as it sinks below the haze —

▼

Mountain ash out the window — another form of life.
Then it disappears from these lines. This life.

▼

Landmarks. The mountains, the inlet, the trees.
The sun. The soul with their names. Seeks
to be entangled with them — oh, not the names,
the others — says she does, anima. But in truth —
no, in illusion, illusion upon illusion, transparent
like glass doors — plays a private game
with words — they're *her* words — like a doll's tea set —
she doesn't want to be any part of the dollies.
She thinks she's grown up.

She doesn't want to be any part of the world.
Outside the playroom, outside the house.

When she admits that, the trees & the mountains
turn menacing. When she insists on that distance,
they recede — go along with the distance —
they become gestalt therapists, they only half-listen,
they say,
            'It's your story.'
                        When she relents
& flows out into them, they accept her, lighten up.
The tree, at least, moves in the wind. The mountain
is purple at the edge, where the sun hits it.

She wants to go to a Rest Home for Phenomena.

▼

The big chestnut tree down the street
    (2nd Ave. & Stephens),
the pavement strewn with glossy brown chestnuts —
It's a commonplace
we're out of touch — out of sync? — with —
with what I could imagine I'd be carried along with —
    (sketchily) —
                so I step over,
or around, each one, on my way to the 2 or 22,
to get to Cap College

▼

The clock ticks — I don't care about nature -
If I have only one happy moment & a kind of
sketch of the external — shape of being radiating
outward from this one of all others, now absent,
but they are the context, they are where the care is,
for them & for me — that I am — most of it let go —
the tree & the pavement & the rain noted, but
most of it not, then what is missing?

4

▼

If I were a man — if this were my city — like — I just heard
yesterday someone on the radio, the AM station, 1130, I found
out about on the Talking Yellow Pages, they have a little ad
for it that comes on before the weather — Lock Your Radio
— the station I turn on to hear if there've been any accidents
— the announcer said 'Capil*ai*no,' like Denny Boyd says old
Vancouverites pronounce it —

▼

Nick's driving
                    along Venables
& I look at the sun
                         this late September
afternoon, daylight saving
                              still 'hangs'
high in the sky

▼

This is being written just after noon on September 22, 1999
— probably the last day of this gentle, warm late summer that
followed a cold, rainy August. I'm perched on a welded steel stool
leaning on the steel counter of a pomo coffee shop which I guess
is called Trees Organic Coffee Co. (at least that's what it says
on my coffee cup — dark Sumatra coffee — the image — the
image of the map — of Indonesia — from the *Globe & Mail* &
the BBC on-line — in mind) — east side of Granville just north
of Pender — this soft bright sunlight off the young maples on

the Mall — light & shadow sharply delineated on the pavement
— to right, Sinclair Centre — the old Post Office — where the
1938 demonstration / police riot still goes on, black-coated arm
upraised coming down on the men running away escaping
down the short flight of steps at the entrance on Hastings St.,
now *Plaza Escada* — dress shop — so are we (tuna sandwiches)
now at lunch time seated at round tables with red & yellow
chessboards on them & painted scalloped edges in two shades
of green, behind a low ornamental steel railing — & people
walking the Mall, two men stopping to talk between the potted
plants, one wearing a madras jacket, hand on hip to indicate mid-
morning ennui — bicycles, buses ... I really don't know what I'm
doing — this is not the world. It's just my take. My lucky take.
My sunny day September take.

Allen Ginsberg said he once dropped acid & went up on a
mountain in Wyoming to sit & experience in sympathy all the
suffering in the world.

▼

Bright light, sharp outlines
                            of September

▼

The boys & girls
                at dawn
Their dawn
                Wipe out
childhood.
                They aren't even young yet.

▼

Take refuge in a long poem.

Avert
      inspiration.

▼

Write carelessly.

▼

On the 210 — tempted now to add a little local colour — as it
lags behind the 4 — now passes — signs on fence — on Powell St.
— *Subway* — &
      Vancouver Today.com —
      virtually all you need to know

& now turns north on Nanaimo — once imagined living here
— near here — near the PNE — all this too thoughtful — write
carelessly, head down, feeling furrow of brow, weight of glasses
— peripherally — sunlit street & cars, shadows, going by — head
up into no thought, even though all this district — no place to go
— the irremediable — gulf — not between being & nothingness

            Angela Bowering
            in Kerrisdale,
            a town

Here is no conflict, no choice — the breeze — the Ironworkers
Memorial — a colour I used to call Prussian blue — Bridge
— the inlet — trees, boats, the forested mountain — bluer
mountains behind — just here

Angela on her last afternoon

spent her last afternoon
with the Finnish genealogists
exchanging information

to be there — by being stop the slide — regretful towards, always
a not-ness, a not there — by consciousness, participating in
the illusion, that doesn't just run one way — entropy — but
has many mansions, some furnished, some just waiting — for
Angela, by insisting on disbelief — to grin. This is not *not*, this is
where *not* is exposed, laid open to view & shown to contain

precise distinctions — almost the 0 & 1 from which 2 arises
— in defiance of pristine order — hors d'oeuvres, instead — start
over

▼

The pleasure of getting on the 7
in the chill morning
                        & something must follow
something non-reciprocal
stuck stuck stuck stuck stuck
all the while the sun — this is still
September (last day) — & the long
shadows before 9 a.m. — is this all —

sometimes the mind
                    is just aware of its
dumbness — the skull — the unnerving
pathos (unjustified, yes, I'll always
scream —

                is that all, just
location, location, location — a grid,
the special sciences
dutiful, perfunctory — & yet a pleasure
not to have any 'meaning' interfere,
long, drawn-out, even before it's thought.
                            Let's be clear
(blank) there's nothing to say here
(quick bump of the tires over the train tracks & now
emerging from beneath the overpass,

& back to reading *Paterson*
on the Granville bridge

        ▼

She wore a red hat. Flat-brimmed.
She wore a flat-brimmed red hat.
It was at Sharon's place, on West 18th.
It was New Year's Eve. Michael Ondaatje was there.
She wore a flat-brimmed red hat & she grinned.

She grinned with delight. With the delight
of disbelief, as if her disbelief had cleared
the air. Like a hailstorm, sweet sun
to follow.

2 FROM VERLAINE

It rains in my heart

It rains in my heart
as it rains on the city
How has such despond
entered my heart?

Soft sound of the rain
on the ground & the roofs
My heart that's bereft
hears the song of the rain

It rains without logic
In this self-damaged heart
There's been no betrayal
Its grief beyond logic

The worst of the pain
Is not to know why
Not loving nor hating
My heart feels such pain

In the interminable

In the interminable
ennui of the plain
the scattered snow
is shining like sand

The sky is copper-coloured
with no gleam of light
You'd think you might see
the moon rise, and set

Like clouds, the boughs
of grey oak trees
in the adjacent forest
drift in the mist

The sky is copper-coloured
with no gleam of light
You'd think you might see
the moon rise, and set

O hoarse-voiced crow,
and you, skinny wolves,
is there anything for you
in these bitter winds?

In the interminable
ennui of the plain
the scattered snow
is shining like sand

5

▼

These things — to describe — not to describe — are important.
That's what I think — I — some voice — not to describe — that
I hear thinking — I overhear. I don't mean to be obscure. The
city weighs tens of thousands of tons — or more — wherever you
look at it — from — motionless. (4th floor of Birch Bldg., Cap
College campus.) Something in your near distance moves — a
leaf — looking over the city then, a cloud — moves very slowly
— there seems to be no weather, no movement of the clouds —
yet ten minutes later it's all changed, invisible winds are pulling
these topographies of condensation out of, into, shapes, though
they look still. But the city is still. It has this — a — not patient,
not impatient — a dead stillness — motionless — nothing could
move it except the earth — to avenge itself — not on us, but on
the city itself — the mere fact of it — being — thousands of tons
of steel & concrete, glass. It's just an image in the eye — it doesn't
exist —

(I've been in offices, in other cities, working, with paper & pencil
& calculating machines, telephones, typewriters, filing cabinets
— & worn the white shirt & thus been in the city & the city didn't
exist —
          no, it's this languour of age that makes it seem to
exist — what's important? Did I start by saying something was
important — that these things that go without description are
important. Description — riding by —
                                        & so there's a mind — I
can't say — & summer's over, the whole latitude is moving. If
it's there as an image — if it's there as inhabiting the poem

— that's important, because it's so for some I, almost random, but
menaced by something that won't die — but that — is in itself
— death —

▼

The city — a block. A little steam rising from one of the flat-
topped high buildings — monolith style — modern. But nothing
else moving. There across the inlet. (I looked to see if the trees
on this side were moving, to give a contrast.) I imagine winter —
the city in the mind — the trees, the branches, waving, blowing
all around, & the rain blowing, but the city still there, dark, in
the mind. So non-existent, that way. There when you don't see it,
as you wake in it. In a bed, in a room, in the city. In one of these
blocky structures projecting upwards — rectangle & triangle
shapes, in rows, among the overshadowing trees, & in them
everyone breathing — separately — or in couples, moving away
from each other now, one getting up & standing, & (the minds)
ready for the day as separate beings — souls — in this structure
— structure of structures — (with its specific history based on
land economy transportation — bringing people in

In 1910
Vancouver then
will have 100,000 men —

& do I think of them as souls? Did I say souls?

building it,
ever more motionless.

▼

Eaton's 'rescued' by Sears —
                    the elderly ladies
with coats & artificial flowers & 'permanents' —
seated on the buses at right angles to the direction of travel —
grey heads, mostly in silence, facing across the aisle —
batting thoughts back —

unburdening minds to high windows — light of the sky —
in the Marine Room at (old) Eaton's —
that gave on the law courts, the art gallery, the Hotel Vancouver,

(now CuiScene — a 'bistro' — no windows —
no crackers with the soup — a 50¢ bun —

        ▼

'Young, but not fresh,' as Lévi-Strauss wrote of São Paulo.
A gray concrete '100' on the grass verge by the concrete viaduct
of the Granville Bridge — monument to youth — to familiarity.

        ▼

So a mind passes through these scenes, acknowledging them,
as also its transitory term,

                    & knowing
all this is important — all
to the souls —

(indiscernible
to each one — they don't know they're here —
& they're happy not knowing

on this bus, fortunate

6

▼

In this time — dark —
the hungry people are sitting in the doorways —
there is no consciousness necessary to this scene —
'how to pick & point & leave them able to change their lives,'
        Jean wrote.

This is nothing they're dying for — the golden lights strung like
    ropes
across Kitsilano — one thing & another —

& Kenneth Koch said, one line crazy
& one line serious —
        'That's OK.'
        'It certainly is.'
        'I'm just going home myself.'
        (missed something)
        'I've got one more trip & I'm going home too.'
        'Might see ya next time.'

One line true & one line —
        cop lights red & blue — flickering fast
        'Are we leaving any time soon?'

One line fast — one crazy & one serious —
would keep them sane & true
& so they could write (New Jersey schoolkids) —

& you don't put the book away
because there's no line pending.

Vancouver is breaking through
your understandable reticence.

Once it's made sure you
were drained of the need
of the will
for everything to be
marshalled

        the city
is not unknowable
it's real

(This is the 10 — westbound — October — dark

7

▼

One among the old people
in the cafeteria on the 6th floor
of the Bay — Seymour Room

Necropolis —

a coffee & danish
not thinking of anything
but the raisins

Sears will manage Eaton's as a traditional department store, not
high fashion, but will keep the Eaton's name because people who
shop downtown aren't interested in garage door openers.

An apartment house in the West End changes hands — 50%
increase in rents — 'All of us could have had strokes.' Not sure if
she read that in the *Province* or heard it on News 1130.

SkyTrain to Waterfront — faces reflected impassive as in an
old T.S. Eliot poem — as if the set of the face belied the interior
mind — and it does — try it — I could teach this to the young.

Wait for something to happen — want nothing to happen.
Homeostasis. Sun flashes past the pillars. Terminus station:
'Will all passengers please leave the train.'

winter comes on in the mind
even before October's half over —
the broom sweeping leaves

In Gastown, the concentric brick circles & low ornamental
posts with chains — what is this all about? Something else than
is given in perception, so shut your eyes. Shut the mind's eyes.
Fiercely.

> No smoking, tourists. Go outside,
> he says. Who? Oh, I forget, I'm dead,
> I can't smoke. Which are tourists
> & which are ghosts.

Look at the old warehouses, concentric circle brick arches over
the windows, pediments with an inset brick pattern & think

> why are there so few
> here
> (compared to, say, St. Louis)

> did they (we) have just-in-time delivery
> from the trains to the steamships,
> the steamships to the trains?

a single ape

in complex light

city of death, city of friends

10 again. Dark, seamed faces,
old clothes. (Some missing word)
as Swedes. This is prosperity.

Washrooms on the 9th floor
Elevator door mirrored
on the inside. Security man:
2nd door to your left.
Mirrors, red & gray tile.
Inside the Hong Kong bank.
It's cool in here, & it's night, & it's not sad.
In the men's room of the Hong Kong bank
(she uses the men's room).

When Debra McPherson pointed over the heads of the crowd
at the anti-TransLink rally & said, 'I've always liked looking
at her,' nobody knew what she was talking about. I knew. She
remembered the stone figure of a nurse executed in high relief
that had adorned the façade at the southeast corner of the old
Georgia Medical-Dental building (blown up) & that had been
repositioned at about the same height on the new Cathedral
Place building that had taken its place.

I saw it on TV. And two days later I read it in the *Sun*. The
triptych of the explosion. A time-sequence. The dustcloud rising
to reclaim the irresolute verticals. I wondered what happened to
the steel frame. Oh, I know now.

The newspaper is held up at a distance, depending on her
eyesight, between the reader and the city or flat on the breakfast
table next to the coffee cup. When the newspaper is lowered, the
city rises again & she forgets that it has changed.

The Devonshire Hotel. I remember when I first came to
Vancouver I used to go to the Dev. They served a great corned-

beef sandwich with hot mustard. I thought, 'This is England!'
Blown up — replaced by — the Hong Kong bank!

Now back downstairs in the (atrium?) she rejoins the crowd
dressy at the opening of a display of photographs of writers. She
sees her own photograph with a poem. It reminds her of Iris
Murdoch's wry inquiring smile before her forgetting.

> These formalities, of people
> kissing, exchanging
> compliments, & lightly patting
> the other's hand, at the same time as
> 'No, thank *you*.'

▼

At Darby's drinking whiskey (that catches the tone of it, no crap
about brands or labels — countries). Watching the Redskins
& Cardinals, from Phoenix, out one eye (the left), & the other,
the Mets & Atlanta tied 1–1 in the 14th, in a rainstorm. The
electronic scoreboard says '14th inning stretch.' And I keep
looking out the window onto Macdonald, the October dusk,
now night, & thinking it's raining here. No, it's raining in New
York, my mind snaps back at my brain. And now from up the bar
voices of three middle-aged lads arguing on two drinks about
Canada & the States. The youngest, biggest, richest-looking one
says, 'There's no sense of urgency here.'

I laugh, soundlessly, smilelessly. No, there's no sense of urgency
here, either.

I'm glad Victoria screwed up the convention centre deal. It means I won't have to walk another 200 m to the SeaBus.

It's not true the snow makes the flanks of the Lions more lion-like; here it is October & the rock is bare; they're like lions sculpted by some Assyrian or Henry Moore. If anything, the snow would obscure these lines.

City of death, city of friends.

8

▼

Crossing Burrard Inlet — many times —
peaceful waters of the mind.

Yellow piles of sulfur, scattering of houses
in gouges, leaning east, on the low hills.
Above them the Lions' majestic
indifference, as if looking away
from the City

                  then the SeaBus wheels round
towards North Van City —
2 red & white Seaspan barges of sawdust —
shadows like grooves in the red sawdust
also leaning east —
towed past —

the sun prismatic on the water — on the eye,
unable to see the page — a blue glow, dazzle
follows the pen

Morning after morning
'the long habit of living'   (Lewis Thomas)
& yet I feel as young as
unconsciousness can

merely part of the mix

Williams would write
a long passage of poetry

interrupted only infrequently
by prose

(& I know I will be back in the thornbushes

no idyl but the weird crisscross
of being & time — only to simply not go
& yet to be bound to go — 'the descent
    beckons' — the privilege
of being part of becoming

not who
I'll be, that's
less important — that's over — you can count on me
not to change — but attend
pub night, the Grizzlies season,

the next time I see Daniel

rather than being
(instantaneously, by magic)
a borderless piece of this sun-charged
air, to drift into a futile mix

unable

▼

What a simple test, that it be interesting
to others. Certainly the mind is, if
it descend far enough

to expose
        the darkness,
which is of most interest to others

(This is a sunny morning, bright fog to the east
on Burrard Inlet — the SeaBus with its flat bow
heading into the slip, all the passengers
in the seats, looking ahead

(& now in the shade of Lonsdale Quay —

Everyone wants to know
what you don't know, or are afraid to know.
There's no need to make anything up. I'll tell you,
and as I do, passing

through this — passing? — heading
uphill, on Lonsdale, on the 239, in the back seat —
& it's not time passing — still
there's a sense of passing, not deeper, quite the opposite, obvious,
    as
passing something from one hand to another, one person,
    relinquishing —

(as if our unwillingness to leave kept getting undermined
by our unwillingness to leave it alone?)
                            did I say, as I pass?

(I won't look back, but let you know where I am,
                        not to locate myself in a landscape
(*Poets in a Landscape*, book about the Romans, Virgil & Horace

(I was talking to
Melanie about Housman — he's more like Virgil than Horace,
the *Georgics* (?) —

not to be noticed, but rather to free the landscape —
relinquishing — my hope for it, a true hope. So let the landscape
be foreground (right now some sense of pale brick & a gas
station) — & let the darkness be the background, let it be ground,
& I'll tell you — it's no big thing, anyway, to be a person, with a
kind of life, yet that's what people are interested in, so I'll tell you
— there's no need to make anything up,

& it's not biography & it's not shame — it is, in fact, the darkness
as a place, an excavation — ongoing (this is something from
Duncan — but I don't know what — don't remember — which
poem) excavation of darkness — of self — of poetry

to bring light into darkness, fashion rooms in caves, collect
treasure because it's treasure, the ordinary taking over, by its lack
of magic denying time — as if it were a puff of wind — nothing
compared to the ticking of the clock which is a real clock (I
bought it in Whitehorse) that sits on the black bedside table

The darkness of the mind & the darkness of death,
& in between the bright day, bright city

▼

This is on the 10 again, about 5 pm, Friday — my state of
mind — the second martini last night got me (but it was soooo
good) — after a day working at the college — office hour,
lunch & teaching — students in groups doing presentations

56

on articles by *Globe & Mail* journalists on 'Between Cultures'
— documentation — my state of mind?

as the bus passes over the Granville Bridge — hazy air — hazy
mind too — a little of the alcohol still — a kind of muteness, as if
relieved somehow of the responsibility of thought —

drink later? squirt? — reading, sleep

▼

Writing in the dark — outside the college — in the sodium
glare through the bus window. In a state of the body — 2 beers
at Poncho's last night, early to bed but wide awake at quarter to
four, obsessing — now the bus moving — downhill — to Phibbs
— all the lights — city dark water reflecting bridge traffic —
In a state of the body.
Spasms of anger.
Obsessing. Yet still at the same time rationally comparing, cause
of anger vs. ? & lying. In bed. Thinking. Brain going. And saying
to the dark, 'I can't stop thinking of this!' (What? Of why the
landlord's rep, John, won't paint the porch, he's had 6 weeks of
good weather. Imagining phone calls. That's when you know
your brain's really got you. Listening to yourself imagining a
phone call. To John. Berating him, no, questioning him. Lying in
the dark. Listening in memory —

Sitting on the 210 at Phibbs, waiting for it to start up, & cross the
bridge. And an hour ago, sitting at the desk while the students
wrote an in-class essay, reading a critical work on Williams &
thinking, yeah, economics, I should have something in here
about economics, the New Paradigm, productivity increases.

▼

State of the body — body in the air — air in the city. 'O my people, stop driving!' I cry, as the 22–Knight goes by, & I'm kept from getting to it by cars making left turns into Macdonald.

So it's Woodward's & Kits — that's the axis, or the power (something) & Eaton's in the middle — no, the Granville Mall, I come back to, the trees, shade trees.

This new — power shift or whatever — to the North Shore — the SeaBus — this is new.

Left brain Capilano, right brain Kitsilano.

▼

Fucking bank machine. Fucking banks without clocks.

And you always have to go somewhere to pee. The Bay, Pacific Centre Mall, McDonald's, the SeaBus station.

But at least here's a bench.

And why should the clock on the Vancouver Block tower be ten minutes fast? & the light burned out on the minute hand.

▼

Why John, the landlord's rep,
has not painted the porch
over 6 weeks of good weather
& now, that it's raining,
lie in bed, obsess. Whom Mrs. B. calls
'the property manager,' or the 'property
management firm' — did B. tell him
not to do it, a false economy? No, no, no,
why would he have told him not to do it,
halfway through the job, with the plywood
nailed down, was it because
I had insisted, was he just trying
to *show me* — & sitting up in the dark, say,
'I can't stop thinking of this — my mind's
a captive audience of my brain, doomed
to hear it out. Brain says —
I'm running this program, & you
just pay attention, lie there. Brain's
on the phone, to John. 'Doesn't this job
ever get to first priority?' And then
another possibility (which I forget now,
some paranoid scenario) — & all the while
mind is listening (& glancing at the clock,
how much sleep lost, when have to get up),
also thinking (on its own, under brain's
hysteria), what's the real reason, &
comes to it — John just didn't
feel like it. Ah, reason! Asleep
instantly

9

▼

Visiting Brian Loomes at UBC Hospital
2 November 1999

He does the same trick with time
that I do, turns away from the 'future'
back to this afternoon that he can treat
like a room, float around in, keep the irreversible
dimension out of sight, like behind a panel,
a piece of dread equipment.

And so he lies
on the hospital bed, not curled up in a ball
around his knowledge, but supine as the Christ,
spreads his hands & says, 'Whatever your cosmological
investment, Mohammed or Motown, I want your love.'

▼

This-ness, now-ness, of the cool morning
& red-green trees

So real, yet without any
special intensity, only inhering
certainty: it won't let me go.

Other times, quick recoil
from a new building seen too often
(detested design),

this time glimpsed through dark
what? more trees? All alone
(as Creeley notes), no connection to this.
Half-folded fist to lips.

(A half-cylinder, oh, ten stories high,
of green glass, like a giant water cooler,
overlooking Larwell park(ing lot),
& you saw it from the Quick Bus office
in the lobby of the Sandman.)

▼

Here I am in this bank without a clock again,
but since it's open, I know it's after 9.

Darkoday is an upside-down sea
of slow-moving cloud backed up against
the mountains, cold & not raining.
Noon.

▼

'You can't fall asleep at the bar.' And the face that turns to me,
away from the bouncer's voice, under a blue cloth cap, eyes
unfocused behind clear-rimmed, thick-lensed glasses, is my face,
middle-aged, roundish, maybe more inoffensive than mine. And
reaches for his beer, the bouncer admonishes, 'No, you don't get
to finish your beer, if you fall asleep. Are you ready to go?' And
the man rises, & turns away, & the bouncer accompanies him,
through the indifferent crowd, under the rainbow-coloured
balloons.

▼

Write carelessly &
stop focusing. I'm in the bar &
James grieving for Michael Hartnett,
there — there in Milwaukee, there in
Ireland. No image, just the tears
& them shed into Benedictine
with a, some kind of monk, he wrote.
(No, a Benedictine monk.)

The mind
edges away
from compassion — imagining
itself compassionate —

                    leave it to the brain,
leave it to the big boy
to feel, even if it
makes big mistakes, it's the big boy,
   it's the one
must
(& I will not say die

I'm in the bar,
I'm happy but I'm lost whenever I come
to this point
of embarrassment as if to take over
knowledge that not yet
exists, is, write carelessly, write
   at the brink
(like a skateboarder I just saw on TV —

wake up! what time is it? —
crash into the oblong
bales of hay — set up —

▼

Writing — to see what turns up, or to keep going. Adrienne
Rich writing for her survival. To keep going, by this means — &
it's not to fake out a justification — excuse — in itself — or is
it? (now the SeaBus passes the stern of *Cielo di Monfalcone*,
Monrovia, & turns (?) sharply right (stbd.), so the whole harbour
seems to wheel around, bringing the Second Narrows into
view, & now the drydocks on the North Shore, & the SeaBus
headed for its slip) — or occupational therapy? That the work be
interesting, & fill (part of) the time.

To survive — those who are dying? To die.
To write without any justification, carelessly,
ah yes. Not to create any structure.
The 239 starts up, at Lonsdale Quay.
Glimpses. Of fog, rain-slick decking,
building, windows, light green siding.

Verlaine's Ride on the 99 B-Line

The Broadway streetscape framed in the bus window
reels backward, halts, recedes again,
turning shop signs to stuttering banners,
as solitary walkers retrogress.
Phone wires & trolley wires loop & cross
with the strange allure of a signature.

The reek of wet clothing, the growl of the diesel
over the fast pulse of its idle
(like the muffled roar of a captive giant),
then suddenly, all around, crows cawing.

What is all this to Verlaine, who sits quietly
in a side seat, the unread *Province* in his lap,
transported by a vision? — a white form,
a sweet, insistent voice addressing him,
while he, in response, murmurs the syllables
of a Name whose cadence quells the bus's rumble.

10

▼

No fear (say the muscle shirts). No fear in the city. It remains a
safe place. A place, then any place is safe, if you are there. (Maria
just phoned. From her place.)

It seems the city sustains — stays the same. (Of course it isn't the
same; when one goes down another goes up. In between is the
vacant lot.

Like the one at Broadway & Maple, that had entered
fiction in a Laurence Gough novel, a gas station & 7-11, blown up
(in the novel), then later, the real one torn down, just an empty
lot with a fence around it.

(At Broadway & Commercial, was that a bank, or was it a coffee
shop? — a low building — cinder block?)

When we were kids they didn't put fences around them. Now I'm
lost. But never lost in the place that is unnamed (even though it
has a name), & stays the same. When you're there, you're there,
it stretches to the ends of . . . a Saul Steinberg magazine cover.
To the horizon. That can be a river, or a desert, & beyond that,
Russia, China. Oz. It goes on forever.

The building at Broadway & Commercial (northeast corner) was
torn down because of drug dealers, now it's land cleared for a
SkyTrain station, & it's behind a fence, & today on the fence
they've hung pieces of murals — or of *a* mural — odd shaped cut-
out poster painted plywood cartoons — images — of the places

that were there before — & a skimpy string of Christmas lights, & it's supposed to be safe.

(The whole place blown up, the gas station & the 7-11, a big bloody shootout over drugs, cars crashing into each other, a driver gets shot & falls out of the cab of his truck into the snow & then the 7-11 going up in a big explosion

                           & yet you go by it, oh, not every day, but often enough (where the real buildings were torn down for some other reason — contaminated ground?). Today, for example, got off the 10 & walked down Maple to 4th, through the block between 8th & 7th where there's no way through for cars (& that's nice too, cause it's different), & across the CP tracks at 6th ...

Safe in the city. Safe because of being in the city, place. & knowing all these things to relate to other things, that don't change, but of course they change & then in between what they were & what they will be there's a vacant lot, but it's not a vacant lot like in childhood, you could play in, & make part of the place you were, it's behind a fence, & now you're old, & you look through the fence that some younger people have put up, to make it safe for you, & you hope (& it's an angry hope, & it's a desperate hope), you hope that really will be (you, that pronoun you hope you are, hope that really will be, & you will be (& then you look sort of shyly away, up the Drive — & all the other old people are there too (where the bank, or the coffee shop, or the bookstore, or the social service agency used to be), next to the fence, standing in ones, look past them & the city goes on & on, outside time, up & down & over small hills, until it gets to the natural line, the water.

▼

Write carelessly, but slowly. Of the place you are, & never fear. Of the fog at UBC, at noon today, not to see through.

At the Ginger & (Chili?) restaurant the server seated me at a large table, to share. Two women found it difficult ordering dim sum without seeing the dumplings.

'Ordinary joy,' that phrase came from the personals in the *New York Review*, but seated in front of me on the 10, the Chinese woman turned to her husband, each of them dandling (!) a red-suited little girl on her/his knees, in joy.

Writing just to get to tomorrow — but today, on the 99 B-Line out to UBC (transferred at Alma), the fog, the trees, grey-brown trunks. (To see reproduced typescript of Ginsberg's *Howl* at UBC bookstore) & die.

▼

Fearing not the muggers or the buggers
but that the city would tear away
from me, leaving only the mind

No, I would not
have any other knowledge (echoes Mariana
in *Measure for Measure*:
'I crave no other, nor no better man')
than this, split
between a city

that goes on (dreamed of,
through the fog, of which I am
indissolubly part — & that is imagination)
& this other dreamless part
obsessing on myself
in which I will not believe.
I will not believe in my own mind, then.

     I learned
(somewhere, somewhen)
the balls & lights on the trees
& outlining the houses
stand for the fruits
of summer. That means
I can look at them & love them
for they are what they are not
& persist in their belief.
The belief that the world has in its own
real time, of which we are part.

▼

'These *Canadian* streets,' I thought, coming back from wherever
I was yesterday, as if I had never been here before. Yes this not
my city I don't want to tear away from merely left gazing at the
inescapable body & mind. Memory of that bank or coffee shop/
bookstore/drop-in centre they tore down to clear land for the
SkyTrain station (see above) — that grimy wall, that had been
there since before I knew it, & the transfers & gum wrappers &
occasional dogshit on the old grey sidewalk.

SENIORS

▼

Gold Ink

Why is the flag at half mast?
Is it for the Canadian security guard killed in Afghanistan?
or the little girl whose body was found in Mississauga?
or Mitchell Sharp?

The flag
1/3 the way down the pole
in front of the firehall
across Balaclava.

The brick firehall — orange brick
(some brown bricks, some red) —
steel gabled roof painted cream
and part of a tree
visible in the space defined
by the walls of the porch
slanting away.
The refrigerator hums, that now I've gotten used to.

Indoors. In behind heavy doors, locked.
Two kinds of locks, electronic on the front door,
deadbolt on my door.

Live with your
self.

One ape —
no, not ape, Stan reminded me — hominid —
though Jared Diamond wrote *The Third Chimp* —
sees himself in the mirror —
recognizing —
it's a reflection!

I live with no self!

No one here but me &
me here because age inevitably has brought me —
I clap my hands & say,
Fukeneh*, it's Canada Day!

for a moment even —
no, for many days,
forgot my age — no —

that no is for real — first word real — I don't know
        what I'm denying. Indoors is
denial — the more denied the better —
just off a boulevard (like Baudelaire) —
reminded of Canada by the flag.

▼

I got an e-mail from Reg —
it said it was from Reg —
'something for you' — the subject line
& the message — 'this is the introduction' —
Security settings deleted the attachment.

I e-mailed back
to Reg to cut & paste. He phoned,
'I didn't send you anything,
I must have a bug.'
                    Viruses every day
among the words —
                    graffiti on the bus —
yesterday on the 9 — graffiti on the rubber flooring
in gold ink — arabesques & bone spurs — drips in the grooves
between the ridges —

unreadable future

▼

I hear the fridge hum, it kind of cries —
the manual says it's a sound like water boiling —
the refrigerant forced
through the coils —
but it's higher pitched. I got used to it.

Also to the soft country/western leak through the walls
 when I'm reading Spanish.
I used to insist more
on silence. Now there's a soundscape. Now I
hear cars & trucks on Broadway.
At night, the lads from UBC
cry out at the sky
when the bars close.

Now I see the flag hang limp at half mast.
The fridge stops. Behind the firehall

the dark blue mountain, white patch of snow —
Grouse Mountain. Delete.

Delete all the false words, not the false notes but
the lying words — the attachments.
Include the music
& all the machines near & far.
Make it a place to die in —
but that's no conclusion, just a true word.

* (pronounced Fuckin A)

Phantoms

Wanking,
don't call up phantoms.
They hang around,

drinking your beer,
sprawled on the couch in their underwear,
pretending to read the *Economist*.

▼

I sent this poem to Stan. He e-mailed back:
'Wanking' is British. How about 'jacking off'?

I defended 'wanking' as 'matter-of-fact.'

(To me, 'jacking off' reeked
of adolescent puritanical shame & defiance.)

▼

I went to Kits library. There, on the New Non-Fiction shelf,
was Ginsberg's *Death & Fame*. In a poem titled 'Jacking Off,'
Ginsberg, 70, regales himself with phantoms:

Who showed up? ... Joe S. .... Huck ... Tom G.
big cocked passed through my dream bed, didn't stay ...

Ah John got you . . . leather handcuffs & strap
  binding hand & feet helpless,
  Leather collar roped to the bedstead's head . . .
Spank good & hard, slap his ass / let him writhe . . .

So came on that unfamiliar fear
  savage control over
  Adonis body, willing
  eager — bound to be true.

▼

The shame & defiance I feel
are my own, not language's –
— and to be so dismissive,
nay, intolerant, of the phantoms –

helpless (yes!) half-beings
that one must oneself become

a half-being
to touch

Seniors

Seniors know everything.
Correction: Each senior knows everything.
The others don't want to hear about it.

Waiting for a moment

Waiting for a moment —
the seniors in their apartments —
at this hour — late afternoon —
the horizon of meaning
is just inside
the living room window —

They don't know what kind of moment
they're waiting for — or they could go out & make it
for themselves — they could move freely about
in the middle distance —

They have no motives — they remember having a choice
of motives — maybe even acting on
unacknowledged motives —
moving here & there — like a thoughtless baby —

Now they have no motives but are still
waiting for a moment —

they know there will be
the right moment —
the right time —

▼

When the first seniors' centres began to appear,
I thought that was such crap.
Looking at the seniors' centre at Aquatic Park, I thought —
my father is an old person, an old man, not a senior,
there is no such thing as a senior,

but now I'm a senior.

I mourn Bruno Klingner — Andy's dad — who died last week
    at 91.
When Bruno was 70, Andy suggested he might spend some time
at the Happy Gang Centre.
Bruno said, 'I don't want to be around a bunch of old people!'

▼

Wild birds fly over the Fraser Valley,
some think they bring avian flu.
Thousands of chickens
burned in big incinerators
on the factory farms
or trucked to be burned in Princeton —
not here, not there,
but oh yes, here, there.

Six hundred slot machines will be installed
at the Plaza of Nations

I put the *Westender* in the recycling bag — just like my father —
finish the paper & put it in the stack — keep every flat
space empty — the floor, the coffee table — cleared —
so the revolving light — looking for a moment —

won't hit any obstacle — any undone thing —
but can look straight ahead to love or death.

4 shortened

The thought has no words, and so no name.
If it had words, it could be given a name.

Is it a presence, or an absence?
It is the presence of an absence.

An aggressive absence, moving in
before its time.

It comes in the afternoon. The 6 o'clock news
is the same as the noon news
but further away. There is more space

for thought. The room is not the same.

▼

Lack of desire. To do something with a guy,
a friend.

And know that these words were so strong
I could live in the world they made.
But that I had made the words myself
to build a world — a world we could talk about,
using the words. To forget it was just raw longing
not to be alone.

              Maybe I'm better
off now, without any common language. I have to
take a chance.
                Words have to come out of the
world (like 'gold ink'). There's no good
flopping around like a fish

or hoping to sneak back into some house of words —
some house of being —

those houses of being are full of hot air
mine is the cold lack now
a being that excludes even me

      ▼

At 5:30 this morning when the fire alarm went off
all of us apartment-dwellers, strangers, gathered
out on the sidewalk to escape the noise —

The cool Sunday morning that had not yet been turned
into yuppie brunch — it had a hundred
directions to look —

It was the cool air, the sun behind clouds —
the street lights snapped off — it was all of us
strangers & no structure.

      ▼

(hungover)

Saturday afternoon on 4th Avenue
cars, cell phones, the din of talk
there are words crashing through words
like ghostly cars

The crowd without purpose
the crowd of cross purposes
that had defeated armies & movements
even the void is not safe
from its reach

And what else — the boutiques, where, Renee said,
the places with the fewest clothes
are the priciest — the women
already sleek & slender selves
but seeking themselves
                                    & home furnishing
stores that were banks —

And among us the old who wear a glimpse of nothing as a face
& everyone passing each other up — people
like cars — thrills of rage if blocked —
even the void runs shrieking from here

take me to where the void
calms down

Common Areas

The common areas are where we meet
but don't meet.

Somewhere I read, or was told,
I should smile.

An error here
might reflect on my right to be here.

▼

We meet here, on our way
from the inside to the outside,
the outside to the inside,
in this place that is neither in nor out,
this common place given for us to use,
coming in or going out.

When my fellow tenant and I are both going out,
we are each going into the world,
into our secret lives.

When we are both coming in that is worse,
we each know the other is going to his apartment,
where he has grave duties to perform.

When one is going out and the other in,
there is a sense of irrelevancy;
this non-meeting might as well take place
outside, on the street.

▼

There are halls and walls
and carpeting.

And the doors that swim by
the eyes.

I recognize the old man
(the other old man).
He gives me a friendly greeting
but a little too quickly.

I give a friendly greeting
too quickly too.

I recognize the couples.

Yearly, they melt
into other couples.

I recognize the burly man in a gray T-shirt
with a big open face
who says hello.

I say hello.

To make an error here —
not to say hello, not to smile —
might lead the other tenant to think
you longed for his annihilation —

to be the only one —
to not have to hide
behind the smile.

▼

There is a stairwell that goes down
past the lobby
to the garage.

There is an elevator that goes down
past the lobby
to the garage.

I have a parking space
but no car.

▼

There is a lobby with mirrors & tile floors
& mailboxes.

There is a door that leads to the street.

When I walk through that door,
the common areas continue.

Corridors
unmarked in air.

Walkers east,
walkers west.

I know this man coming towards me
(with the glasses & ball cap).

There's no reason I should dislike him
just because I've seen him
so many places,
so many times.

It's like he was another tenant

but a tenant of what?

▼

Would heaven be
total anonymity?

America

I've been doing, no, writing, this so long —
nothing wrong.

▼

Now the words tell of something so obvious
as to see the air in front of you
but not to have known it was something
to see.

To find it is America, still the same,
streets & houses, along the way,
all individual lives & dealing with it —
all this time —

as if a time never changing —
to come back to this place,
lived in together, only, that's all —
each dies

& the one who dies is only dead for a day,
no one says they're dead, they just say *was* —
still they are with us only they don't know it.

Knowing one will enter that *final* being,
not sleep, not death, not the eternity Emily was

appalled by — but America — always home —
come back to & never gone away —

all this writing never thinks of having an end —
to walk down the street for no reason but to be in reason —
in love in a way —

going to Chicago —
relying on nothing but — on nothing but —
being alive

11

▼

At Sausi's. At the bar. A guy in a T-shirt & shorts stows clothes strewn on the sidewalk into bags, some marked with a company (or agency) name, which I can't make out, some plain green garbage bags. He lifts the bags into the back of his truck. I'm looking into the back of the truck so I can't see the logo on the side.

So I wait. He's lifting the last bags in now. Parking light on his truck on-off. Big trees.

▼

Sausi's is closing. To be replaced by a Banana Leaf. Reterritorialization.

They close September 30, so they're holding their annual Oktoberfest in September. Septemberfest.

We'll have to find some new place to drink.

Car alarm.

▼

'It looks like it's going to rain.'
Smart kid. He's already looking at the sky.

Barbara Munk said she would miss the sky.

▼

the mere presence of beauty
unexpected against the ordinary
(arising understandably & naturally out of the ordinary)

▼

At the Lennox

4 boys who cannot get girls (I think)
but are not gay (I think)
4 of them
at the bar but ordering pitchers.

Maybe one of them is gay.
The one next to me
with the earring.

(I hung out with a bunch of guys
in 4th year high school
('buncha guys')
& one of them turned out to be gay. Well, two.)

Not a horseshoe
but a small semicircle of gold
tipped by two small gold balls.

Fall falls.
A change in the relation
of background to figure.

The walls & windows seem to draw in,
the figure more alert,
more aware of
her
life.

▼

In the dream I lamented the passing of bistros
like the Modern, which was Sausi's three reterritorializations
     back
(bistro, fr. Russian *bistro*, fast).

I imagined a restaurant: Fishtro.

'[My brain] is wondering how it thinks. It ought to know.'
                                                    J.M. Keynes (age 6)

▼

Late at night
they shout into the night
at not comprehending
how this happened,

breaking into
the sleep of the winners.

▼

They lie on the concrete.
The winners go by.

a cap, a cup

▼

C. reminds me that the Modern was also the Bavarian. Café on
the left, restaurant on the right. This and the Budapest (4th near
Alma) were the restaurants Robin and Stan — and I — went to
— late 60s.

▼

Every time there's a stabbing or a mugging,
check the address and plot an imaginary line
that moves
westward & northward.

▼

Tree roots lift & crack the pavement
asphalted over bulges

Tabloid & mini-tabloid sheets scattered
on the double-hexagonal pavers, amid yellow leaves

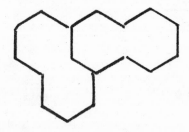

or like this

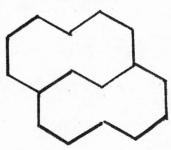

or two octagons yoked by a square

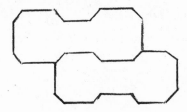

a toonie for the young guy

'In old age you don't choose the language you speak in.'
— Milton Hatoum, *The Brothers*

▼

The man at the bar at Mark's fiddling with some kind of
electronic device has a half-filled glass of red in front of him &
a half-full carafe of the same. Then up comes his buddy & says,
'Are you winning?'

▼

What is my relation to this city I am not at home in? And from
what angle to expose it so that maybe I could fall in love with it?

Expose some side of it as if the city were a man but not my man.
Who is he Vancouver?

▼

to turn over (as if in bed)
and expose
the side of him who is
Vancouver to come

come from Alberta to the Drive
(the future of Vancouver is to come from Alberta
has to come

to begin
the exposure

this is true. As if turning over in bed to find
the back
of the man who is Vancouver
face hidden

from Alberta

working in construction

non-union?

▼

interanimation

▼

I went looking for him at the Hudson, Granville & Dunsmuir. I thought he might be dancing on the high steel, in sneakers.

This old lady.

No longer any bare steel. Narrow glass windows, up top concrete floors. Live-in work spaces, advertised. The old bank entrance façade preserved behind green shrouds.

I got closer. Opening & closing umbrella.

Couldn't get any closer. All Visitors Report to Site Office. And is this Earl's behind me? No, Dubrulle International Culinary Arts. Reterritorialization. Not to describe.

Somewhere downtown Earl's is.

Now I'm out of the rain, under the whatdoyoucall it, overhang? — glass & steel — awning? — of Canaccord Tower, I can see easier. Inside second story, first over rectangular, deep caverns for retail, behind glass, white hardhats & raincoats, two. Moved away from window.

▼

Or up the street, in the 900 block, where Blaine Culling once planned to open two grand restaurants, one Mexican, one Russian,

(past Granville Books gone),

two sites: one modernistic, unfinished, glass shack,

one huge cavern, green girders (bus blocks for a minute), one
man maybe a foreman no hat, one other watch cap, sit, drink,
talk on cell. Back of me heavy bass from Caprice Lounge once
Caprice Theatre

(& all in between Robert Graves' picture of Britain in the '30s)

(& I notice peds don't allow for notebook held horizontal writing
on projecting from body sensing how close to pass — you have
to watch it)

▼

19 October 2005. The Banana Leaf painted Sausi's the colour of a
banana leaf.

'While ninety-nine in the hundred who never attend the banquet
Must wash the grease of ages off the knives'
　　　　　　　　　— Louis MacNeice, 'Autumn Journal' (1938)

▼

The banquet was at the Shaughnessy Golf & Country Club.

We went up by tables.

Hors d'oeuvres, then the baron of beef, then desserts.

I was sitting with my friends.

We never did meet the bride's family.

This is where the Premier hangs out.

The boy is asleep outside Banana Leaf. (Later, he'll move on.)

The shaggy man has two spots for his cardboard, outside Safeway and on the south side, near Starbucks.

The boy gets a toonie.

The shaggy man gets a toonie.

Barb Munk wrote about the Garbage Can Man.

Barb Munk died (and the minister said, 'We don't have her any more.')

It all goes on in the mind.

There's just this day.

▼

28 October 2005. Received two pieces of mail, one from CONDOTODAY, one from VIDEOSELF.

▼

Daylight Saving Time ends.
I hope they've stored the daylight
somewhere safe. I hope they've invested it
at the going rate. We'll need it when it comes.

Late afternoon darkness
between slats of living-room blinds
closed but still admitting
an image of lights & rain
in thin lines

The buses move like shadows
blotting the lights

Abbey Lincoln's 'Strong Man'
smiles between each kiss.

Impressionism gives out
so take one step back
into the mind

and the next move is to the heart
the semantic heart
not knowing what it knows

no help from the body
looking out the window

▼

'puke green (which some might call chartreuse)' — C.

▼

At Olympia

Happiness
on either side:

fam-   ily   3   persons
of   4   signing

on screen hockey fights

Newfoundland Labrador choir

takes first in Spain

all under 16

their plane will 'touch down'

'and it'll be Beatlemania'

From one construction site to another

▼

Here on the 99   murmur

standees (who's standing them?)

(going to east side, to look at chapbooks, check out design of
    at People's Co-op for *Seniors*)

black-clothed November   white sky

cheered at recurrence of clouds in Joel Sloman's *Stops*

Granville, doors open, in, out

stroller face blocked by dark head

dreads   white Banana Republic bag

Denny's (where we picketed non-union in 1972 or 3)

Toys'R'Us over BowMac

BCAA anti-gay
no, sorry, anti-transit

it doesn't matter what I write here

electric razor building   my dentist

Tojo's tiny servings   (with Daniel)

Willow, in, out

stroller face sucks thumb apricot jacket over pale blue GA might
    be COUGAR

blocked again

standees hang to·straps it doesn't matter

        ▼

children and old ladies
dressed alike
bright padded clothes
Grey Cup semi-final

I don't care.   I care.

Crowds

after Baudelaire, 'Foules'

Not everyone can take a bath in a crowd.
Only the one a fairy has breathed on in his cradle
can get a kick out of the crush of human immersion.
Only the one with a knack for cross-dressing
and masquerade; only the one who hated his home.

Multitude, solitude: these are equal, reciprocal terms,
for the fecund poet. Unless he knows how to welcome
invisible guests to his solitary musings
he cannot walk untroubled through the busy streets.

The poet can be at once himself and another.
Like a wandering soul in search of a body
he can enter, at will, any person's emotions.
For him alone every door is open,
and if some seem closed, they aren't worth his time.

Solitary walker, solitary thinker, he gets drunk
on solidarity. The crowd's embrace is for him a joy
denied forever to the egoist in his walking coffin,
the mollusk-man in his giant shell.

The love men speak of is tiny, feeble, stifling,
compared to this indescribable orgy,
this saintly prostitution of the soul

giving herself completely, *poetry and charity*,
to the unexpected happening, the stranger passing by.

Teach the so-called winners of this world
(if only to bring their stupid pride down a notch)
there's a happiness greater than theirs, and sweeter.
The poet must sometimes laugh at the ones who deplore
his patchy career, chaste life.

12

▼

Army & Navy no longer carries men's blazers or jackets — I've
been looking all over town — in the consignment stores (haven't
yet got to Value Village (V for veracity — the loss of the vera city)

Liam sent me this mouth of truth, Bocca della Verità (postcard),
from Rome (I took it just now from the bookshelf to copy — that
— now I replace it — that gazes — now I look at it — dumbstruck
or appalled at what it sees

▼

The ones walking & asking
a full-grown man
rage readable, patent.
You wouldn't be surprised if he hit you
as hard as he could.

a man with no money

not even a cart
(the new entrepreneurs)

a man with only his meaningless arms & legs
meaningless hands

you better have some change on you
as soon as he

but he can't ask for change

▼

But every so often or not
you run into one of them
who says, with a shy pride,
Yes, I was born here

I was a librarian
at Tupper

and you disappear into the present

▼

Augie & me
sitting on a knoll
with numerous older others

I'm licking a mango gelato cone
we're watching Scottish dancers
on a stage at the PNE

warm sunlight, sounds of joy
from Playland,
living in a country at peace

But is Canada at peace?
Four soldiers have been killed in Afghanistan,
identities not yet released
(heartstrings tauten
from here to Halifax)

civilian

▼

(Life. Money. Balance both.

Scotiabank)

▼

The mouth of truth
is cracked at the bottom.
It is adorned
with a flowing moustache
with an ornament, a kind of seal, below the nose,
a seal with an incised triangle, like a tepee,
against maybe a hill, bird or insect shapes
    ascendant on either side (or just scratches).
It has not spoken.

Deep in the mouth is the word it would speak
but now it is transfixed
with horror with fascination
with what is going on.
With us, yes.
And its left eye is cracked, too,
so it seems more like a cavern than an eye.

The guy is gassing up the fire engine.
When I look at him,
I am the mouth of truth.

▼

Word On the Street

A low roar in the background,
the swishing sound of traffic.
Vancouver will continue on in peace,
undeserved, no, deserved,
by the ones with no guile in their hearts,
no time for guile —

lose your need
to be one with (them)

when the clouds
drift, the sun shines
like a word

sudden, rays
off the buildings,

& lifts you to the sky
like a word — it's not something
    you need to have known
aforethought

The sun, the sky,
are thing-like
so is the body
thick or stumbling

lacking
no romance of it

▼

What was taught in those large classrooms,
large-windowed, big, imposing schools
(Bayview, General Gordon)?
the dedication,
despite the truth, the pain
in each young, ageing mind

▼

Two men push loaded carts
one behind the other, on the street,
not the sidewalk, outside the line
of parked cars. A third, dark, bearded,
watches from across the street.

You pass one of them coming toward you, pushing,
& you know you can't speak, you know
caste
here

▼

How does it seem
the people on the bus
are not of one people
(the Bus Riders Union
has tried to appeal to it)

The guy riding his bike
coming up behind pedestrians
on the sidewalk, silently
not of one people

not of one city

▼

Sit at the Tank
outside, you with your friends who smoke —
that's still allowed —
& sip a Jamie, knowing
it's this time, no other, this transparent
collision of times, of times flowing through
    each other

times with their inside stories

▼

Crossing Macdonald:
'Excuse me, sir.'
(no answer)

Reaching the other side:
'Could you give me some change, for a hostel?'
(Digs in pocket, finds the toonie, the large coin, by touch,
withdraws hand from pocket, places the coin
in the other's palm (no word. no eye contact.)

'Thank you, sir.'
(silence)

(resentment, anger)

They should be sitting by the wall.

▼

He doesn't know where he's going,
no, he has nowhere to go
so puts his big steps one
in front of the other
to the street corner.
He stops, thinks
where to seem to be going.
(Portland, from the MAX)

▼

('Experience open living. Vancouver style redefined. This
is SWELL, 47 modern flats on Broadway at Quebec, where
the city's hippest residential, creative and downtown
neighbourhoods connect. A prototype for intelligent design
in a locale that is ultra-convenient and uber-chic. Think fresh,
flexible and everything essential. A study of poetic and spacious
practicality contained remarkably within.
                                        from the $300,000s')

▼

Is that huddled mass a person?
No, it's not large enough.

It's a person's belongings.

▼

At the Tank

— I can't believe they're going to cut down all the trees.
— Thirty-five to forty percent.
— That's horrible! Who voted for this?
— There was no vote. It's the Planning Department. They held
  public meetings. I went to two of them.
— And was anybody against cutting down the trees?
— Yes. Almost everybody who spoke. But the city said they have
  to do it because the tree roots are heaving up the sidewalks.
  And they're going to get rid of all your pretty pavers too.
— To be replaced by what?
— A brushed concrete pavement.
— A what?
— A concrete slab, with a broom dragged over the wet concrete
  to make ridges, so you won't slip when it rains.

— Could they not have trimmed the tree roots?
— That over budget.
— O.

— Sooth, the city did ask the merchants if they'd put up some
  bucks for a more costly renovation, but sooth, they said no.
— O.

(Council passed the Street Rehabilitation plan
but more than that, asked the staff to go back &
'report back to Council as soon as possible with options &
    budgets
for sidewalk treatments which:
Retain a higher number of existing trees . . .
Allow for future installation and maintenance of large trees . . .
FURTHER THAT staff replace those trees that are absolutely
    required to be removed with specimens that will match the
    existing Linden canopy')

    ▼

Pensioners, among the mysteries
(kick along leaves
that, wet, would stick to their soles),

the street in their minds, too,
the mysteries in the private quarters
surrounding the mind —

thoughts that lost their language
thoughts recognized just by bumping into them
occasions of fear or lust
or lust blocking fear

a territory we will keep until someone has
    some other use for it
that will keep us, tracking each one, until

it has no time for us

The mind is this street
only the interiors
around it
arranged
differently

Vancouver, 1999 – 2007

Notes

p. 4. *The Tin Flute*: Gabrielle Roy's 1945 novel.

p. 5. 'In all the beer parlours ...': Ian Tyson, 'Summer Wages.' Florentine: the main character in *The Tin Flute*.

p. 13. 'The Woodward's Beacon ...': Bruce Macdonald, *Vancouver: A Visual History* (Vancouver: Talonbooks, 1992), p. 39.

p. 36. 'In 1910 ...': Tourist greeters' song. Alan Morley, *Vancouver: From Milltown to Metropolis*, 3rd ed. (Vancouver: Mitchell Press, 1974), p. 149.

p. 45. 'Sears will ... keep the Eaton's name': It's now Sears.

p. 55. *Poets in a Landscape*, by Gilbert Highet (New York: Alfred A. Knopf, 1957).

p. 111. The phrase 'invisible guests' is from Czeslaw Milosz, 'Ars Poetica?', *Bells in Winter* (New York: Ecco Press, 1978), p. 31.

Acknowledgments

Blue Canary, The Capilano Review, Chanticleer, Dooney's Café, Fras, I Saw Johnny Yesterday, Insurance, It's Still Winter, The News, The Poker, Rust Buckle, Sal Mimeo, Shampoo, Shiny, Tolling Elves. Parts 1 and 2 were included in *At Andy's* (New Star Books, 2000). *Seniors* was published as a chapbook by Nomados in 2006.

Other New Star poetry titles

ANNHARTE *Exercises In Lip Pointing* (2003)

STEPHEN COLLIS *Anarchive* (2005)
  Mine (2001)

PETER CULLEY *Hammertown* (2003)
  The Age of Briggs & Stratton (2008)

MAXINE GADD *Backup To Babylon* (2006)
  Subway Under Byzantium (2008)

ANDREW KLOBUCAR & MICHAEL BARNHOLDEN, EDS.
  Writing Class: The Kootenay School Of Writing Anthology
  (1999)

JUSTIN LUKYN *Henry Pepper* (2008)

DONATO MANCINI *Æthel* (2007)
  Ligatures (2005)

BARRY McKINNON *In The Millennium* (2009)

ROY MIKI *There* (2006)

LISA ROBERTSON *Debbie: An Epic* (1997)
  The Weather (2001)
  XEclogue (1999)

JORDAN SCOTT *Silt* (2005)

GEORGE STANLEY *At Andy's* (2000)
  Gentle Northern Summer (1995)

SIMON THOMPSON *Why Does It Feel So Late?* (2009)